GiO and The Cookie Dough MONSTER

Written and Illustrated
by Steve Morrone

To Jenn and my girls, Sophia and Nina.

This is a story about Gio and his Mom,
he was a good little boy and he was usually calm.

You see Gio would get hungry
and eat everything in sight.

For a little guy,
he had a HUGE appetite!

He loved to eat SWEETS from the "Sweet Stuff" shelf,

but his favorite
was the COOKIE DOUGH
that Mommy made herself.

He could watch her make

COOKIE DOUGH

all day long,

but Mommy said stealing some
would be wrong.

If she turned her back
to do something else,

She'd turn back around
and see his little grin,

and she could tell by the cookie dough
there on his chin,

that he was sneaking some anyway
even though she said no,

and saying "but Mommy
I didn't, I didn't eat the dough."

This one day Gio's Mommy
walked away from the table,

and Gio was a good boy as much as he was able.

She said as she left
"DON'T YOU EAT THAT DOUGH!"

"I should be able to trust you when I go!"

Then he thought to himself,
"Mommy's always saying NO,"

So he **dabbled**
and
nibbled
and pinched off some more,

and soon,
there wasn't as much **cookie dough**
as there was before.

Suddenly the cookie dough began to RUMBLE!...

it jiggled,

and Bobbled,

and WIGGLED,

and GRUMBLED!!...

It started to **glow** and began to rise
and Gio couldn't believe his eyes!
Suddenly the dough stood up on two feet,
'twas the **Cookie Dough Monster**
That Gio did meet!!

"Alright Gio I've had just about ENOUGH,

of your pinchin'

and your nibblin'

and the REST of your STUFF!!"

"Lying to your Mommy
seems to be your plan!"

"Look you've got COOKIE DOUGH
right there in your HAND!!"

"It's time for you to tell her what you've been **doin'**!"

The Monster said,

"I ain't STICKIN 'round
here no more!"

and with a wiggle and a stumble,
he ran out the front door...

The Cookie Dough Monster
took off with a
ZOOM!!

Gio's Mommy was entering the room.

"Gio!"
she shouted,
"You've eaten all the dough!"

"But Mommy, I didn't,
I really didn't though."

Well, this time she was angry and
sent him to bed.
Gio stood there and stared
at her and said,

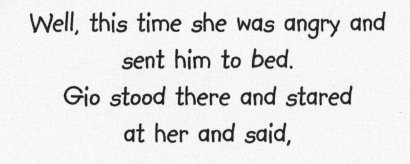

"Mommy, I mean it,
I won't eat
any more."

But she sent him to bed anyway,

because he'd done this before.

As Gio thought back
to those tiny little lies,

There was sadness
growing in his eyes.

"I have to do something to make it all better, maybe it will help if I write her a letter!"

So he started to write down
how sorry he was,
for making Mommy angry
for the bad things he does.

Dear Mommy,

I'm sorry for lying about eating the dough,
I should have listened to you when you told me no.

So I am telling the truth now so we can be friends,
and you can start to trust me again.

I love you Mommy and that's for sure,
and I won't steal cookie dough anymore.

Love,
Gio

Mommy found his letter
    the very next day,
and she knew right away
what he was trying to say.

He was beginning to realize the meaning of trust,

and telling the truth to your Mommy
is always a must.

The end.

CPSIA information can be obtained
at www.ICGtesting.com
Printed in the USA
BVOW10s2316210316
441222BV00005B/8/P

9 780692 626054